FIERCE
DAY

New Poems ❧ *Rose Styron*

◆ FriesenPress

Suite 300 - 990 Fort St
Victoria, BC, Canada, V8V 3K2
www.friesenpress.com

Copyright © 2015 by Rose Styron
First Edition — 2015

Cover Painting: *Shining Tide*, oil on linen, 14" by 21", 1985. Kib Bramhall

All rights reserved. No part of this publication may be reproduced in any form, or by any means, electronic or mechanical, including photocopying, recording, or any information browsing, storage, or retrieval system, without permission in writing from FriesenPress.

ISBN
978-1-4602-7480-4 (Hardcover)
978-1-4602-7481-1 (Paperback)
978-1-4602-7482-8 (eBook)

1. *Poetry, American*

Distributed to the trade by The Ingram Book Company

Also by Rose Styron

Poetry
From Summer to Summer (Viking, 1965)
Thieves' Afternoons (Viking, 1973)
By Vineyard Light (Rizzoli, 1995)

Translator, Contributor and Editor
Modern Russian Poetry (Viking, 1972)
Poets on Streetcorners (Viking, 1975)
Unholy Ghost (William Morrow, 2001)
Letters to My Father [William Styron] (LSU, 2009)
The Selected Letters of William Styron (Random House, 2013)

for you

☙

That in black ink my love may still shine bright

Poems

TODAY   1

ICE   2

SQUIBNOCKET   3

RASPBERRY VINES   4

SHADOW   6

ROXBURY: JANUARY   7

LAST NIGHT   9

TO ASHES   10

VETERANS DAY   11

TOWARD DAYBREAK   12

DECEMBER 24TH 14

TURKS & CAICOS   15

FEBRUARY 14TH 17

ALARM OFF   19

LEAP YEAR'S EVE   20

ALONE WITH YOUR LETTERS   21

BEACON HILL 22

NORTH ROAD 24

HIGH HEDGE LANE 26

LUCY VINCENT BEACH: LATE WINTER 27

SLEEP LONG LOST 29

PACKING UP 31

OCCUPY VINEYARD 32

EASTER: LITCHFIELD COUNTY 34

4/20 36

4 A.M. 37

6 A.M. 38

APRIL IN GEORGIA 40

IN THE GARDEN 41

WAKING IN CONNECTICUT 42

WALKING 44

FAMILY SWIM 45

A MOMENT IN MAY 46

LILACS AGAIN 48

6:30 A.M. 49

7 A.M. 50

SUMMER SOLSTICE 51

GOLD SNAKE 53

TOWARDS NOMANS LAND 55

CEMETERY: LITCHFIELD COUNTY   57

BELIZE (FOR PETER M)   58

SKY   59

FINGERNAIL POEM (*AFTER MUIN BESEISU*)   60

PUSHKIN SQUARE   61

GOING   63

VINEYARD HAVEN: OCTOBER   64

NOTE IN A BOTTLE   66

LUCY VINCENT BEACH: ANOTHER SEASON   67

BLIZZARD   69

TODAY   70

ACKNOWLEDGMENTS   73

ABOUT THE AUTHOR   75

POEMS

TODAY

You would have loved today,
sharp winter sunshine, new windows,
too cold to take a walk.
Cardinals in the empty branches.
Eider ducks on the Sound-edge sand.
No place to go. Books
open to their final chapters. Mozart
by the fire, lighting
our endless world. The house
straightened at last.

ICE

The tanagers turn south.
The chill rain sets tiaras in the trees.

I think of you as snow in sun,
a bell for clear blue soaring.

Let me be. I do not find
your image on the wind.

SQUIBNOCKET

A score of terns. Another score
come whirling, whisking off the shore
this solstice daybreak where the sun
now rising wands them one by one—
white, winged, airborne, gowned
for ceremony, orange-beaked, ebony-armed
to catch the dazzling fish that live
beneath the water where I dive
silver around me—
thieved

secrets, love, last long.

RASPBERRY VINES

Loss—
and the willow bends
still green in November
and raspberry vines bear
surprising sweetness
under this tardy frost.

Where are the cardinals
going and the cranes?

Thought, light
on a falling leaf
lulled by the silky
haze, at first rain plunges,

meets the slick black
highway everywhere
leaf upon leaf,
as twilight loses sky.

Yet not a drop has spilled.
Love is its fullest.
It follows leaping
with deer by the brook,

gliding with summerwind moths,
leading moons down the
rivered lane.

Love in November is
counting
cows slowly crossing a
country road,
afraid.

Death has time.
Will the willow hold
its weight,
will cranes or cardinals turn,
your footsteps turn?

SHADOW

Later in full moon when you walk
out from this pungent vineyard
where we share
the maze of thickets
the sheltering arching vines
and then
the rays through leaves—
roof-dense, electric, flickering, and in
inconstant shadows
walk the brilliant beach,
run the night-sand
as it cools, towards moonset, wary only of
the lightstruck tide—
will you remember fear? take care of
fear? What will you follow home?

ROXBURY: JANUARY

Awakening, high
in our writers' house
the desktop empty
the sun still low

a bowl of clementines
coffee's rise
Egyptian dog out
testing snow

we await the master
who sleeps too long.
A white-gold morning
teases, but it is not

daybreak's song.
It is not the signal.
It will not bring him home.
How shall we raise him,

how fill his cup
with love, heat, memories,
a country muse's
promise of spring—

the sun full up?
Child, come with news,
trance him for one more
beautiful page

that honors his sadness
or vivid youth
or wild black fantasy,

pride in age—anger—the world's—

in sickness, truth.

LAST NIGHT

We were the family
there on his bed the five of us
touching his arms, his chest,
cradling his head.

Four children
bending to
him, to ease his departure, bless
his mysterious

journey—
then I alone
uncovering the bony legs,
preparing him for rest.

Now I, in the limbo of
our fashioned earth,
cannot remember
how to be

alive,
crossing abandoned fields,
edges of cracked white sea,
high priest of sky.

TO ASHES

A tisket a tasket
they've put him in a casket
to ship him off our island
to burn his spirit free.

Standing in the deep sand
(quicksand) near the ferry
I'm distracted for the hour
by such absurdity.

Autumn summons winter.
There is no way back.
The trees will bare at sunrise,
the birds all black.

VETERANS DAY

Bluebird across the graveyard sky,
the burial begins—

the Buddhist prayer,
the Christian hymn,
the singing swinging low again.
We lower your ashes carefully,
your son, your
kin, strong love.

Then Taps.
And now the young marine is gazing up
at bits of sky
through shovelfuls of fresh
rich earth, rose-strewn—
and now the eager young marine
is left alone
under a blanket of drying grass,
wet snow, and all these blossoms strewn
too soon.

Bluebird across our graveyard sky,
orange breast catching all the last bits of light,
sing that the burial begin. Sing.

TOWARD DAYBREAK

All night, all crowded
alien night it seems
I wait for sunrise's rescue:
the band of coral light
heralding, touching the dark
windows on my sea
the black crows flying up
against the slate
blue suddenly
and the fourteen black/white ducks
almost a Valentine
lining the frilly edge of tide,
shell hearts along the curve of sand.

At last, the sun
brilliant as full moon summer's eve
far to the right now
behind the bare chandelier
of our tree, upside down
as my world
without you—gone
into a thousand early mornings
that stretch across thick-tiered
horizons here

clotted gray-blue, only a penciled
rim of yellow light beneath.

I wait impatiently for the sun's
reappearance, high above this
window in the white-blue paper
sky—holding up the land, the
far side of the harbor, the white
slant gulls, white papered desk.
Day again. More day. Fierce day.

DECEMBER 24TH

The world tonight is clear,
if only for an hour

Orion's belt encircling us,
the far indigo ocean
thundering near

and I remember
rain in the alley
no shortcut home.

TURKS & CAICOS

I've lost my pen
and in the act
I've lost my way.

Was it deliberate
not daring to record
this strangest day?

Pure beach. Long walk
as sought, but
sudden end—

view through the dangerous
coraled grief-waves blocked
beyond earth's bend.

Turn back?
Fix frigate birds
in the white sky?

Push on, passing perhaps
some warrior test

while the tide's high?

Frost-like I'm caught
before each
green-starred choice.

Drown all regrets.
—I hear you. Still,
which is love's voice?

FEBRUARY 14TH

Valentine's Day,
our first apart.
Are you not coming back?
Where do I put this paper heart?

The snow, the sleet last night
this morning's year
whites-out our world.
They said you'd reappear

once I let you go
got rid of history's mess
(the noise, the clutter I created)
said you'd return to bless

a quiet life
share it again with me
lend me one more swift chance
to perfectly

tell you how long I've loved
and not let pride
or fear from decades past
lure me to hide

my need, my hope
or lately, fresh desire.
Strange: those weeks, our words,
how you'd admire

some silly thing I'd done
outfit I'd wear
fresh thought or
my unruly hair.

Earlier seasons, you had not,
but now you'd say
over and over,
as that day

in ancient Rome: *I love you.*
What wild sweet flight
what daring ride we ended.
Was I right

to let you go? How can
the earth make sense?
Chilled cardinals huddle here

and lightfooted horses
black-paired at our fence.

ALARM OFF

Bluejays flash in the windowed tree,
swans set sail by the dock,
a timeless winter morning shines
defying the heart-set clock.

LEAP YEAR'S EVE

Crisp white snow
on our dark green firs

heart lights gleam
an owl spell stirs

full moon on fire
this leap year night—

gift: one day more
for love's last flight

ALONE WITH YOUR LETTERS

At your desk
this cold unbeautiful dawn
I sense blood flowing
from your pen to paper to

your keen self unfound—
we could have searched together
had I been brave enough

to enter those black rivers, black.

BEACON HILL

I have inherited your dreams.
What is this foreign Beacon Hill
we stroll all gaslit night?
Amos and Andy radio voices spar
window to elegant window
across the narrow cobbled streets
by Louisburg Square—
villages of Virginia, ruins of Rome
rolling away.

We are slim, fit, eager,
exploring New England's darkness
for the first time—no dogs,
children, lazy sun or pilgrim fires
in sight. Presidents Kennedy, Johnson,
Reagan, Clinton go by in cavalcade
down Charles Street at the bottom
of the hill. Each pauses, waves.
You hurry closer, give them one by one
advice for the world, in oratorical tones:
its horrors, distant, coming closer
slave and prisoner of every hue
burned, beaten, under cross and star
fleeing, coming closer, standing

in the dock, hugging a tree's shade
coming closer, seeking, somehow
a paradise of justice.

The carriages disappear.
On the corner, a boy from the old South
plays marbles in the dirt yard.
Amos and Andy, Brahms' Alto Rhapsody
soars, ends. Deep silence
pierced by a bully's senseless tirades
refuses to let me wake.
An old tyrant's words echo
refusing to let me wake.

NORTH ROAD

Zen wind
carves through us
climbing its unseen path. At the top
sky-crashing February,

brown-iced leaves underfoot,
bare splayed branches,
the stunted oaks.

But here's a patriarch red cedar—
horizontal branches layered,
still dark green.

Light through its moving
branches breaks in shadows
the whole landscape, even the sea.

Now, sun-defined, a smooth white
double beech,
dancers caught together,

heads lost in Italian clouds.
Last Saturday on Lucy Vincent Beach
we found their kin

fallen from the cliff,
heads down, tangled, whispering, curly,
faces completely in the sand.

They held our weight
all afternoon
anticipating a harder tide.

HIGH HEDGE LANE

Winter and I have come again.
Snow on the lawn, snow on the beach.
Dockside a startled gull,
six eider ducks not seen before
explore the February waves.
Sun crowns the cardinals.
Berries, the holly.
A house is being built
next door, entire.
The hammers ring,
a tuning fork in the cold air,
carrying the workmen's voices
and their laughter, as it rises.
Unexpected music.
I am not alone.
Perhaps a wedding on their lawn,
their new verandah,
perhaps neighbors
bearing garden roses?

LUCY VINCENT BEACH: LATE WINTER

Our landmarks gone.
Rough violent winter
gouged the golden sandhills
collapsed the grassy lookouts
from the top, the wooden benches,
platforms to descent. Parachutes
would be the best way down today.

Here, below, walking along the mid-tide
strand, I see—broken, buried—
the stairs we'd climb post-season
to see the world from absent strangers' lawns
imagining lives in their old high houses
hidden behind green blossoms, branches.

No slime-sweet pits of clay halfway up.
Now even the horizontal birch tumbled one September,
smooth white trunk we'd sit on
watching the sea forever, gone.

Sun-miracled February morning,
unexpected calm,
I stop at the sea-edge now,

the sea-carved sea-washed boulders
I stand between—

Once on this treasured journey
not so long ago
these rocks, invisible part of the sand-cliff then
created shelter for our picnics,
coves we hid in, not
watching swift June couples, dogs and children
pass a curious whale or dolphin
poking its head above the waves.

Each landmark gone
flashes in the homebound mind.

Low tide.   A life going out.
How soon   back in.

SLEEP LONG LOST

but keep out light
preserve the dream
your eyes closed tight
pen, pad, stay near
for you must write
and the habits: dark—
stay wrapped in night

a little longer

don't face day
too early.

How I used to
welcome morning
sunny, rainy
golden, pearly
rise, prepare
the gorgeous day
before you—man, child—
woke to say
good morning.

Now I cannot

leave this bed
shades down, my once soft
pillow: lead.
Yours empty, and our
dogs still dead.

On Upper County Road
the peepers sing—
weeks late, and leafless still.
Our walk held Spring.
Bright worlds might soon arrive
too early.

PACKING UP

Okay. Time to get on with it.
April's fool just tossed his velvety
cap, and the little point-bells
from Shakespeare's
stage a chorus with our own
windchimes in Connecticut.
I am invited to join at least
one more spring circus here.

The poetry hour. But first
crocus, witch hazel, daffodil buds
and untamed forsythia: yellow time,
the sun's. Stale bread and lemon
cake crumbled for the nuthatch,
robins, song sparrow at the window-box.
Blue jays and squirrels beware
when I bang on the glass.

OCCUPY VINEYARD

April wakes our island
white pear trees bloom and bloom
along Clough Lane
through Sunday rain—
Does God hear churchbells chime?

Is He asleep as we have been?
Let Spring's alarms remind
all we've not done
to clear the sun
and purify the land.

Alarms beyond such beauty sound:
dead mallards (seaside lawn)
no roses (fiercest winter's storm)
entangled fish. Dark smoke trails form
where child-drawn clouds moved on.

May's comedy: these fresh green
boughs mask broken fence
and awkward limbs
(Siberian elms').
We smile, applaud such chance

to sally forth again, again
surviving one more hurricane
counting now each blossom, wing
beats timed as citizen voices sing
soar and descend, atone.

EASTER: LITCHFIELD COUNTY

Easter's come in hyacinths of glory
gone the way of crocuses, first daffodils,
late snow, the children and their
children we have sprung

also the scores of rainbow eggs
the small hands dyed and we
conspired to scatter in our special
places on the sunny greening lawn.

Daylong they ran, tumbled and compared
cellophane baskets full of treasure
sang Happy Birthday to our
Easter child: fair Martha

you will never hear.
I missed you at each window watching us,
hidden in your study through the day.
With each small hand in mine outdoors

I'd spot your eye-sent brilliance
turquoise, magenta, sparkling orange still
to be discovered in the crooks of aging trees,
cracks in the steps, in terrace cushions,

crevices of our wandering stone walls,
in the woodpile you tended before you
lit each evening fire, in drainpipe mouths,
budding flowerbeds, roots of old

forsythia and twisted grapevine,
the Italian arbor, Russian lilacs,
house of our history's secrets
held between us, brighter, holding on—

4/20

Anniversary: Father's death.
I was not there then
legend years gone by.

Today it's you I mourn
Love
my life's companion.

How this dawn
their absence—all great men
our hearts have, even
in denial, known—
weighs down.

4 A.M.

What shall I do, afraid of day?
Find words you gave me, hold them tight?
If worlds knock, call, what should I say?
Can't seem to make a friend of night
as you supremely might.
Bad dreams hold sway.

6 A.M.

Eyes closed, denying creeping dawn
after the usual late damned night
I heard
    too close in my
        window tree
three cluster notes—a nameless
        bird—
call me.
Eyes closed, I feared, I wished,
    it you.
Could I recapture, if I chose
to rise before the sun I knew?
If only I could memorize
his song.
But then, the moments passed
and soon a different song—
    a bell
pierced my window
then a trill
a separate bird
a name stills.
If I could memorize
and name each song

could I recapture you?

Open my eyes?

    Not long

        for what I cannot

            longer be?

The mourning dove
now calls in close
    those distances it ferries
        now—

APRIL IN GEORGIA

By Ann's spring pond
where I awake
tall water iris lean
lavender, secret
yellow hearts
opening, unseen

till bumblebee and butterfly
black, yellow
sun-parts shining
startle our perch
alight each bloom
all fear undermining.

IN THE GARDEN

Bluebells, like Martha's scalloped costume sleeves
are pirouetting on their childstems—April wind.
White andromeda spread their elegant
lace fingers, peach azalea umbrellas the
lavender, creeping phlox
and the first viburnum
buttons white its shawl.

In the close green cove where we sit talking,
the children and I, low purple violets open
even as we watch,
bleeding hearts bend, early grace.

So many shapes and shades of green!
The doubted life returns,
beauty in diversity—
lawn, flowerbeds, hedges, arbor, feathery pale
branches and the rich full leaves of maples,
birds nesting
in their small dwelling.

How could you abandon life
amid such glory?

WAKING IN CONNECTICUT

Amazing morning—
every tree and bush
bursting greenly—

weeping cherry
in the Japanese garden,
lilac fountains skyward
now over the pond, now low

at lawn's rim,
white dogwood stretching
beyond the old stone walls,
plum, pear, cherry, magnolia

dropping petals, scattering
their wedding trails, receiving
bluebirds mating, nesting,
one flying now to greet

or warn me
as I descend the lawn,
and stop under the willow
thirty feet high at least

we planted together long ago
to celebrate, remember, and resolve.

WALKING

I stopped to pick a simple spray
of white mock orange
of white spirea (Spring! today!)

where gold red berries last were hung
in mourning

FAMILY SWIM

Reflector-bright red waterspider
navigating star
swim across that bluest edge
and back to where we are.

Have you sent your babies
to the swamp edge in Iraq?
Before they're poisoned, poisoning,
stop them. Please keep track

of who had begged to go or not
hitched rides when much too young
to learn protection, to protect
each innocent spider lung.

Now you advance. Should we retreat,
our little ones and I?
Do we dare to let you climb
our shoulders, star the sky?

A MOMENT IN MAY

There is a moment in May
when quince and jonquil turn the lawn
into a color mart.
Attractions for each age, a stand
for old desires. Andromeda
poses by the yew,
the fortune of forsythia hovers
where tulip-darts, their target missed,
stick in the ground
and early apple blossoms beckon
precarious for us
as the stone-piled wall.

Bounded by stillness,
by wall and white cottage and the
tall kuzura tree we
planted together
when this patch of lawn was
every season and the only world,
our eyes measuring the tree's
peak, the height of a sudden
sparrow, we recall:

it is a moment, petaled, lighting as we
light from the past,
to bless us dark and far on our
many winds' way.

LILACS AGAIN

June: French lilacs
lavender and prim
follow our wild white
beauties lost to May

as later lovers
circumspect and trim
follow escaping angels.
I would stay

high on that whitest fragrance
yearlong were it not
that each fresh bud's an
arrow tip, heart shot.

6:30 A.M.

Rain last night, confounding
the stars we bedded down.
Across the mica harbor-tide
grey wool East Chop stretches,
a forgotten skein.
Just now
it wove itself together, wore
a pale yellow collar, combed
its wispy length of cloud beard.
Sky's priestly face appears, is turned
toward morning
blue linen after all.

7 A.M.

The lawn belongs to the birds this morning.
First of July, wide sunlight opening
across the grass, two white iron chairs
huddled daises,
somersault rosebush, raspberries
that await my pruning.
From the porch chaise, sun-striped, I observe
day's progress. Do not interfere.

Down by the hedge the fat crows gather:
Blackshirts, ready to pounce.
A pair of pink-flanged doves nods
to the preening robin. Under the eaves
of their freshened summer houses—chestnut
locust, elm—multiple jays and heraldic
cardinals their noisy visits start:
on their own verandahs
gossiping over berries.

SUMMER SOLSTICE

Suddenly,
there's nothing to do
and too much—
the lawn, paths, woods
were never so green
white blossoms of every
size and shape—hydrangea,
Chinese dogwood, mock orange
spill their glistening—

Inside, your photographs
and books stand guard
in orderly array. Your
half of the bed is smooth,
the pillows plump, the phone
just out of reach beyond it.

No one calls early—they
remember your late hours.
The shades are down, so
sunlight's held at bay
though not the fabulous winged
song of summer birds

waking me as ever, always in our
favorite room, our season.
Yesterday's mail on the desk
newspapers, unread. Plans for the day
hover bright out all our doors—

Don't think of evening.

GOLD SNAKE

November. Still
our isle reels gold.
Maple leaves that catch the wind
shake
tree and lawn
its wide green cloth, its
gold-rimmed floral china strewn
under some globed sky.

Sunrise out the abandoned window
(how I star-tired dimmed to sleep)
wakes the Sound—
stray swan, pale sand grass
dahlias nodding by the wall—
and spotlights:
Snake.

(What dreams unfold
luring me down
the gates of day to keep.)

Gold snake atop my garden wall
just as dawn in Vineyard Haven
haloes East Chop, I

in thrall to sunrise always
plunging waveward
racing shorebirds in crescendo, free,
shiver, stock-still, shadowed
watch your tongue flick, savoring air
watch you, shadowed, snaking inland
gone from sea.

Golden moment that still slithers
snake, you slither under ivy
through some creek I have not found
yet though I follow

golden snakeskin now.

TOWARDS NOMANS LAND

From the sun to me
On the rim of the world
the highest dune
    on a cattailed cliff-edge south

sun, prince of the afternoon
a shimmering golden caterpillar flung
    in tapestry
    across our sapphire-woven sea

and wingprints of a charcoal
flight of terns
and filigree and ribboned beach
    binding the priceless cape to sky's enamel

antique emergent beauty of November
throne and Sunday, flung to me.

Unbearable
to see it, then, withdrawing
    slowly, of course—with prince's dignity

or whim, call it what you will,
the sky bluer than ever, radiant pins.

Inland I turn
and walk awhile
    trace casual gorse, hard red
berries on the empty path, thick slopes,

    arrowheads, inheritance. Sudden: cicadas in applause
set me round
swiftly, while there's still
light, time, trust

time to gain the imperiled cliff
again. Disappearing:
    the magnificence of apricot
    persimmon, gold

into the far off grove. Aladdin's lamp
shines on the rim of the world
tonight, bright rim of the one
world farthest from me.

CEMETERY: LITCHFIELD COUNTY

I walk though birches white and gray
over the graveyard's back
to catch the sun on an icy slate
etching a name by winter's light
I loved when this hill was golden, gay
and the young deer left no track.

Perfect in snow, Connecticut
conceals each chasm and rock
charcoal branches draw the eye
upward from memory to sky,
but still my heart in slate is cut
and the river, still, is black.

BELIZE (for Peter M)

The mysterious forests
cecropia, palm
their enchanted
creatures of shade

deep vinewound paths
mud python roots
spiked crowns
the bromeliads made

awaiting the moon
or a skittering bird—
dark loves
but no more for me.

The passions of age
are for lupine fields
sun's road
and a shorebird sea

SKY

A balanchine of white doves whirs
over the Gay Head sand this noon:
a ballerina troupe
soaring the updraft wind.

Sudden: from the dune grass
three great swans swoop
shadow our upturned faces

(as higher past those ashtrees
Tsvetaeva loved, departing
the cranes of sadness
shed white feathers,
emptied all our skies).

Which angel is it in the corner frame
calling the Annunciation?

FINGERNAIL POEM (*After Muin Beseisu*)

on the windowpanes
on the porcupine's skin
on the curtains
on braids
on the plates in restaurants
and the hats, buttons, rings
I wrote this poem.

In the night, when the newspaper's
proofreader died
he dies without reading the proof.

I wrote it in coal
on snow
and on new shoes
for the ink has become like mud
and the paper, how miserable the paper is!

PUSHKIN SQUARE

Pushkin
on his pedestal is sad.
From Moscow to Chicago,
Paris to Damascus,
Capetown to Saigon,
lovers cry out to him
"Sing, sing for us, Pushkin!
The world is mad.
No one can hear our song."

From Harlem to Havana,
Lima to Prague,
in snow-laced Leningrad
lovers cry
"Give us your land!
Fiercely we'll guard and glorify
it as you taught us.
Trust us. Trust us."
Lovers are never wrong.
The world is mad.

Through parks of iron,
forests of bone and chain,
lovers are crying,

"Find us, Pushkin, sing for us,
unhinge the door!
Our view is honor
but we miss
each other and the trees
and all those promises."
How long we've had
trysts to keep under your hand.

GOING

Leaves like terrestrial bodies fall
each morning where my dazzled mind
lies, sifting through autumn sand
what's left of loves,
counting their gallant shells, and still
denying that its right to summer end.

Brightness to brightness moves
but on the strange path we travel
the sky now smooth and civil
and the shaded wall
hiding no fine mansion but graves, graves
can we trace the sun in the scarlet maple?

VINEYARD HAVEN: OCTOBER

A light October afternoon
wind ruffling
the sky at four
empty of shorebirds
of footprints.

Try not to define
the point on the horizon
where the Shenandoah all too soon
should disappear.

Try not to remember
how fragrant and what shades
of green and white clematis vines
trembled, the breeze at dusk
early this year.

Try not to make notes
for future poems where love
—tangled, swept on the autumn
sea this hour—will lie,
a coral atoll in the sun's glance.

Let the wind
though the wind be north
and your body tensed
for storm and desolation
blow through.

The sheer cliff
shuts summer out behind—
lawns, children at play—
an invalid's closed window—

and the sharp shadow of man

loses to light,
and you cannot keep pace
and the ships you have laden
together sail far, far
their prows to an unseen horizon.

Try not to describe
too well, thus hasten,
the weather of mourning,
their going, love's.

NOTE IN A BOTTLE

Whatever you may hear,
I care.
Life is too wrung with chimes and brass
applause for me to face,
though I would trade
the medals that I wear
for lace.

Whatever you may doubt,
trust my despair.
Yesterday my love was caught in a throat
of fears,
by tongues and ears,
its own tide,
beset.

Today I tie
a ribbon in my hair
and keep a diary of regret.

LUCY VINCENT BEACH: ANOTHER SEASON

Vast sandmeadow where we used to step
so carefully on the entry path
between the stones or rust-nailed
driftwood or the prickly bushes

and now at the water, hulking
cliff and cave that blocks
our easy passage further
battered into prehistoric shapes,

black craggy column to the sky
pocked arch from nowhere
stretched behind, sheltering a huge
white boulder fallen only yesterday

and through the arch in sudden sunlight
wind-carved horizontal layers of earth
terracotta stripes like doorways
in a seaside town: Minori.'53:

a balcony, a chimney, water trickling
somewhere, and no way round again

even at lowest tide.
Terminal moraine.

We seek and climb another path,
above, down, down and see
a stretch of water never here before,
a hidden opening to Greater Chilmark Pond

a view to Black Point, Quansoo,
Abel's Hill and all South Beach stretching
in sun to Edgartown, the length
we fast-walked once, and later

strolled, in lambent times.

Tonight, the full moon shimmers.
This vista is enough.

BLIZZARD

Listen the midnight wind
is rising in our harbor.
The moon's impaled
on triple-pointed branches
of our winter tree.

Shall I go out to it?
And climb, and snatch its light?
Swing high toward morning?

Here it comes now
pulling its sheerest bedsheet
over my roughshod mind.

*

We're almost there
gold ring suspended in the air

and yet I'm slowly falling.
Are you falling?

Where?

TODAY

You would have loved today,
this twilight
high in the wild-fever
spring bruised field.
Straight young lilacs stand at the
edge and hidden
sentries in the cattail stalks
and buttercup, daisy, Queen Anne's lace
in the stray breeze nodding.
Rim of the heart
first redwing blackbird calls
in the tall sycamore.
A pair of bluebirds swings in the windy
elm.